TOADSTOOL!

An Introduction

To Edible Wild Mushrooms

Of New England

TOADSTOOL!

An Introduction

To Edible Wild Mushrooms

Of New England

L. A. DeFusco, M.D.

ISBN 978-0-615-36346-2

For Jake,
my father

CONTENTS

Preface ix

Introduction xi

What Is A Mushroom? *And* What Are Toadstools? 1

Spring Surprises 5

Sumptuous Summer Finds 17

The Pause That Refreshes 31

Autumn Adventures 35

Other Delectable Goodies 45

The Bonus 49

About Poisonous Mushrooms 51

Practical Considerations 55

Glossary 57

Mushroom Nomenclature 61

Bibliography 63

Preface

When I was ten, my dad took me, along with some cousins, to a property in Connecticut, owned by a farmer he knew. He got the word that there was an abundance of mushrooms there. There were many oak stumps, streams and sufficient shade to support fungal growth. Also, there had been a lot of rain during the early days of autumn. The stumps were loaded with mushrooms and you could hardly walk without stepping on them. The vast majority of them were honey mushrooms and I could hardly believe our good fortune. We picked until we became exhausted from the effort, and it seemed as though when we thought we were through, there were more and still more. We had to remove the 2nd and 3rd seats from the '41 Plymouth "beach wagon" to make room and mushrooms filled the wagon from the back of the front seat to the roof and all the way to the rear. After giving away many of these, my mother "put up" over 100 quarts in Mason jars. Although I was never again to see such an enormous quantity of mushrooms, my lifelong love of them had begun.

Introduction

If you enjoy roaming around in the out-of doors or like to hike along forest trails and take in the beauties of nature, I would like to invite you on a three-season foray for some of the best edible wild mushrooms. It won't cost you much, just some time, mostly, as you escape from 'civilization' to be among the many wonders that are just waiting for us to come along!

The mushroom season in New England effectively begins in late April and extends to early November. The species vary with the calendar, although there is considerable overlap. Join me on an adventure into the world of wild mushrooms.

I am not a mycologist but a retired OB-GYN. This is not a textbook but rather a primer for anyone who would like to learn more about wild mushrooms.

For a number of years, during my education to become a physician, I did little mushrooming. Once I hung out the shingle, I resumed my forays and have done so almost every year, and more frequently since retiring. It's so satisfying to do something you enjoyed as a youth. Everyone does this to some degree. We bring joyful experiences of the past with their positive emotions into the present. It adds continuity, fullness and well-being to one's life. Surely this is how traditions are born!

There is a peacefulness that settles on me when I'm in the woods looking for mushrooms—a feeling like this is the way things are supposed to be: natural. And then to come upon a cluster of choice edibles is like finding an unexpected treasure. And they are free! We get so used to paying for everything; it's a treat to get something for nothing. Even when there are few finds, I thoroughly enjoy being amidst nature's flora and fauna and the opportunity to appreciate "things as they are in themselves,"[1] undisturbed by human endeavors.

If you are new to mushroom hunting,[2] it is most important that you

---

1 *"Indian Summer"*; 1857, Adelbert Stifter, as quoted in *"The Curtain"* by Milan Kundera

2 Don't know why some people call it mushroom hunting. I never have seen one try to get away!

go with someone experienced for there are dangerous, even deadly, mushrooms. Joining a group such as the CVMS,[3] an affiliate of the North American Mycological Society, is an excellent and safe way to learn more. At each of their forays, which are held weekly, all of the fungi that are brought back to camp are identified by experts. CVMS also sponsors lectures and workshops. The members share their mushroom foray experiences, recipes, pictures, etc. Their quarterly newsletter keeps the members up on what's happening in the world of mushrooms.

There are many fine texts that you can consult—see bibliography—and their pictures and identification techniques are very helpful, but there is no substitute for having an experienced mushroomer with you. Some texts have artist renderings of mushrooms but I consider these a poor substitute for photos of the real thing, especially in their native environment. Even so, one should never rely solely on a picture to identify a mushroom because many mushrooms have poisonous "look-alikes"! Still, there are some very fine mushrooms for which there are no dangerous ones that remotely resemble them.

We'll begin our journey with the optimism that the new growth of spring inspires and as the weeks and months proceed we'll be encountering prize after prize right up through the floral foliage of fall! Foraging for mushrooms costs little more than the time one invests while the healthy outdoor activity and the culinary delights that follow are priceless.

But first, allow me to explain just what a mushroom is…

3 Connecticut Valley Mycological Society

What Is A Mushroom?
And What Are Toadstools?

I've never seen a toad use a mushroom for a stool, though some people, especially those who would never eat a wild mushroom, use the word "toadstool" when referring to any mushroom. Actually this word implies inedibility or toxicity and there are many fine edibles for which "toadstool" is inappropriate. The mushroom aficionado almost never uses the word toadstool but makes it his business to know which mushrooms are edible and which inedible or poisonous. More on poisonous mushrooms later.

Foraging for food, an ancient tradition, is deeply ingrained in us since it was essential for the survival and success of our hunter/gatherer primate ancestors. For those who enjoy store-bought (usually cultivated) or restaurant-served (often wild) mushrooms, learning to forage for their own wild mushrooms will add a whole new dimension to their appreciation of them. It is to these people that I address this presentation.

Mushrooms, once considered to be plants, were included in the Kingdom Plantae, but now have their own kingdom—Kingdom Fungi. Besides desirable and not so desirable mushrooms, this kingdom also includes such fungi as molds, rusts, yeasts, smuts and mildews. About 100,000 species of fungi are known.

All living things, including humans, belong to one of the five kingdoms.[4] All have a blueprint for their life processes contained in their DNA,[5] which carries the genetic information. So, in a very real way, all manifestations of life on this planet are related.

You'd be amazed at how much DNA humans and mushrooms have in common! In fact, we now know that we humans share more of our DNA with mushrooms than we do with plants.[6] Would you believe

---

4 Some taxonomists prefer six Kingdoms or three Domains and, more recently, seven Kingdoms have been recognized, but this does not affect our discussion

5 desoxyribonucleic acid, the principle constituent of chromosomes

6 Baldauf, SL and Palmer, JD 1993 Animals and fungi are each others closest relatives—congruent evidence from multiple proteins. PNAS, USA 90: 11558-11562

that humans and mushrooms had a common ancestor about a billion years ago?

Unlike most plants, mushrooms do not have the ability to photosynthesize and must, therefore, absorb their sugar from the organic material[7] in their environment. Because the mushroom cell wall is largely composed of chitin, a chemical which forms the exoskeleton of arthropods (e.g. insects, crustaceans), the organic material must be broken down before it can be absorbed. This is accomplished by enzymes secreted by the fundamental cellular element of the mushroom, a tiny filament known as the hypha. As a by-product of this activity, mushrooms play a very important ecological role, for by decomposing organic matter they return nutrients to the soil and prevent huge build-ups of decaying organic matter. Lignin, the "skeletal" tissue of wood, is broken down by fungi better than any by other organism. Lignin is also found in all vascular plants.

Some mushrooms, with their underground connections to the rootlets of plants and trees, form symbiotic relationships for the benefit of both. These mushrooms are called mycorrhizal and their contribution to the relationship is through their mycelia, which are aggregations of hyphae. While most plants and trees have these relationships, it is also true that the majority of plant and tree diseases are due to fungi!

When we pick wild mushrooms, we are removing the spore-bearing fruiting body of the fungus, whose function, via the spores, is the production of more mushrooms! Most of the fungus remains hidden underground or in decaying organic matter. This substantial part is the vegetative part of the mushroom. Although some fungi reproduce asexually, sexual reproduction is the norm among those mushrooms that concern us.

In the 18th century, Carolus Linnaeus, a Swede, created the binomial nomenclature and made it his mission in life to name all living things—an impossible task—identifying each particular life form by genus and species, in Latin![8] We are still doing this today.

Human beings belong to the genus, Homo, and the species, sapiens, to which the English word sapient is related. Since sapient refers to one who exhibits great wisdom or sound judgment, I am

---

7 organic material—carbon containing nutrients derived from living matter

8 *Systema Naturae*; Linnaeus, 1735

sometimes puzzled at its application to our species! I will use the common names in this presentation, but the Latin names, corresponding to the common names, are presented under " Mushroom Nomenclature" on page 61, where the mushrooms are listed in the order in which they are presented in this work. This will be helpful when seeking further information on any particular mushroom.

In the 19th century, Elias Fries,[9] also a Swede, applied Linnaeus' system to mushrooms as he named many of them. Fries laid the foundation for modern mycology. His classification was based on the morphological characteristics and so he grouped similar appearing mushrooms together. He also emphasized the value of taking a spore print. See page 8. Many more mushrooms have since been identified and named, although, even today, there remain many unidentified mushrooms.

Charles Peck, in the late 19th century, used the microscope to examine mushroom structure and their spores.[10] He also noted the effect of ammonia on a Boletus illudens specimen. Peck, the New York state botanist for 50 years, named more than 2500 mushrooms, and has been called the father of modern American mycology. Spore examination and responses of mushrooms to various chemical applications are both still used as aids to identification and classification.

These pioneers—Linnaeus, Fries and Peck—all shared a static, unchanging view of life. This contrasts with our present-day understanding, thanks to the observations of Charles Darwin, that all living things are continuously undergoing change, i.e., evolving, albeit slowly.[11]

It seems that similar appearing mushrooms, a la Fries, is a flawed effort in defining relatedness because like structures are now thought to be the result of convergent evolution. That is, similar structures evolve because different mushrooms are exposed to the same environment. Of course, this like response to environmental stimuli also suggests relatedness!

For the past 15-20 years, DNA sequencing[12] has been increasingly

---

9 *Systema Mycologicum*; Fries, 1821
10 cf. mushroomexpert.com by Michael Kuo for his excellent essay on taxonomy
11 *On the Origin of Species*, Darwin, C., 1859
12 biochemical method used to determine the order of the bases in a DNA molecule

applied, among other efforts, to revealing the common ancestries of mushrooms and an ongoing reclassification of fungi into "clades," based on their common ancestries. This has led to an amazing correspondence of grossly dissimilar mushrooms. Linnaeus, Fries and Peck must be rolling over in their graves!

I hope this introduction gives some perspective as to where the magnificent mushroom fits in the scheme of things. Let me assure you that you'll not be needing a microscope, nor will you need to learn any chemistry. And you surely don't need to be concerned with DNA studies, interesting though they may be. So hold on—the meat of the mushroom story is about to begin!

Spring Surprises

MORELS

Blonde morel

It's true: in the spring a young man's fancy turns to…mushrooms… as well as other delectable beauties! Morels are among the choicest mushrooms of spring, growing from late April to early June. They are easy to identify with their honey-combed architecture, but not so easy to find—and those mushroomers who have their spots are not likely to share this info with anyone. This slow-growing mushroom may develop over several weeks. True morels have caps and stalks which are hollow. False morels, some of which are poisonous, usually have a chambered interior and their exterior appearance is bizarre as contrasted with the regular architecture of the black and yellow morels.

The black morel appears earlier than the blonde (yellow) morel. They are often associated with conifers and can be easily overlooked amidst fallen pinecones. These firm mushrooms can be washed without fear of them becoming water-logged as gilled and pored mushrooms often will. And they must be washed because all the fenestrations in the cap make convenient hiding places for tiny "critters." Morels are not usually found in great abundance in Connecticut, where I usually forage. In the east the yellow morel outnumbers the black and is associated with deciduous trees. Both black and yellow morels are frequently found in recently burned areas.

Morels are popular in the Midwest, especially in Minnesota and Michigan, where morel festivals are common. The yellow morel is the state mushroom of Minnesota. This morel is sometimes referred to as the "May mushroom." Unlike the majority of the mushrooms in this presentation, whose spores are on their gills or within their pores, the morels have their spores within tiny sac-like structures called asci.

I wasn't much into looking for morels, primarily because I grew up on autumn mushrooms and then, much later, developed a passion for summer mushrooms. One day a friend, knowing of my mycophilia, called to say there were some strange looking ones in her backyard. Her description told me what they were and I advised her that this was a wonderful find and asked what was she going to do with them? Now many people are reluctant, even afraid, to eat anything found in the wild, and rightly so, unless one is certain that it is safe. Anyway, she said "I don't want them, do you?" Do I? Cleaned and sliced and sautéed in butter[13] with onions, these blonde morels were a wonderful addition to dinner. There is nothing quite like eating freshly picked mushrooms! Because morels are hollow, they are good candidates for stuffing. More on stuffing mushrooms later.

---

13 Clarified butter (drawn) is preferred for sautéing. It's less likely to burn because the water and milk solids have been removed. It's made from unsalted butter.

OYSTER MUSHROOMS

Oyster mushrooms

I don't know why oyster mushrooms are so called. They don't look or taste like oysters. Perhaps the oblong shape of their caps and the lateral attachment of their stalks bears some remote physical resemblance. This interesting gilled mushroom has the potential to grow *all year round*, even during a winter thaw. They are often found in great abundance and present many appearances. Often the stalks will meet at the point where they grow from the tree or stump. They are associated with deciduous trees and their color intensifies during the cooler seasons, varying from white to gray to brownish hue. The gray oyster resembles the cultivated oyster sold in grocery stores, but is firmer, as are the brown oysters. Sliced thin, you may sauté them or, when quite firm, marinate them in oil and vinegar. A marinating technique is described on page nine.

The "green oyster" is a firm green-yellow autumn mushroom, very firm; it is best marinated. Like many mushrooms, oysters may grow in the same place the following year. However, one cannot count on this and their appearance in any given area is often a total surprise.

The flat crep, an oyster-like mushroom of unknown edibility, should be avoided. This mushroom tends to be smaller, lacks a stalk, and is easily distinguished by its brownish spore print. Oysters have a white to pale lilac gray print. I do recommend one learn how to do a spore print. It's easy. After cutting off the stalk, place the cap, gill or pore side down, on white paper. Cover with a glass, and, after several hours to overnight, the spores will fall onto the paper. Although an impressive print may result, we are only interested in the *color* of the print. (The color of the gills—or pores—is not an indicator of the spore print color.) Along with the anatomical features, this is an aid to identifying the mushroom and although it cannot tell you the identity of your specimen, it may often tell you *what it is not.*

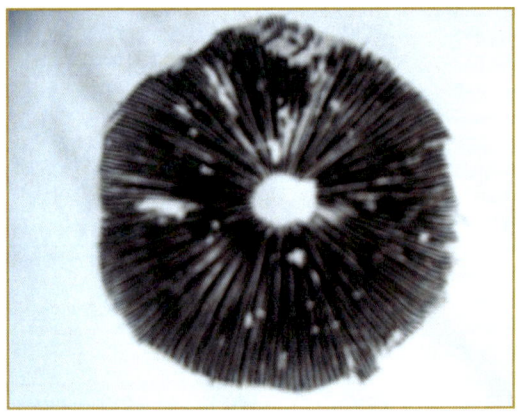

Spore print

Very young specimens may not have sufficient spores and very old ones may have already lost theirs. White spores can be difficult to see, but with a hand lens or with black/white paper, this is not a problem. A simple hand lens is also very helpful when examining some of the more subtle anatomical features, such as the manner of gill to stalk attachment, the presence of fine scabers, etc. The spore print above is obviously that of a gilled mushroom. If you are comfortable using a microscope, you can scrape off some of these spores with a cover slip and place them on a glass slide on which you have added a drop of water and examine the spores under high power. Spores from differ-ent as well as similar mushrooms can look very different under the microscope and this can further refine the process of identification. In the field, however, the most important tool for proper identification remains an experienced mushroom hunter.

White oyster

Angel wings, an oyster-like mushroom, is another fine edible. Their caps are delicate, thin and soft, and if not harvested when optimal, are prone to become water-logged and/or infested with insect larvae. Nevertheless, when they are good they are great. I enjoy them sautéed. They are found on decaying conifer wood. Angel wings lack a stalk and are a fall mushroom, for the most part. Its spore print is white.

Marinating is a great way to prepare all firm mushrooms—honey mushroom buttons, hen of the woods, the chicken mushroom, and many others. This is how my friend, Fortunata, does it:

> To one cup of wine vinegar that has been brought to a simmer, add 4 cups of blanched mushrooms. Stir for 2-3 minutes. Place in colander and drain off the vinegar, by placing a heavy weight on the mushrooms and pressing down manually and firmly to express the vinegar.
>
> In a separate bowl add chopped raw garlic, chopped jalapeno or cherry pepper, oregano and basil. Season to taste. Add 1 tbsp. vinegar and mix. Add this to the mushrooms, along with extra virgin olive oil, and mix again.

Put this in quart jars and pack down firmly with a wooden spoon until 2 inches from the top of the jar. Add extra virgin olive oil to one inch from the top. Be sure everything is covered by the oil. Seal the jar tightly. All should be accomplished while the mushrooms are hot. They will keep indefinitely.

The succulent caps of the oyster mushroom are a scrumptious choice for stir-frying. Cut in half-inch strips and stir-fry in a little olive oil and/or butter along with hot Italian peppers for 20 minutes or so and then if you add in some onions and stewed tomatoes, you will produce an unforgettable dish.

THE CHICKEN MUSHROOM

Chicken mushrooms

The chicken mushroom is a strikingly colorful polypore that can be seen from a long way off because their "shelves" are yellow-orange to red on the upper side. The under surface is sulfur yellow. These mushrooms can also grow quite large; in excess of 15 pounds is not unusual. This also makes it easy to spot. The mature chicken can hardly be confused with any other mushroom.

The immature specimen is the best to consume. These are much smaller, the shelves less defined, club-shaped and mostly white with minimal orange coloration. Also called the sulfur shelf, this fungus is found on both deciduous and coniferous trees, from the base to heights necessitating a ladder. They are also found on trunks, logs and buried roots. The sulfur shelf has a long growing season, May to November. Young specimens, though more digestible, are found less often because of their smaller size and less vivid coloration. Sauteed with butter, onions and topped with fresh parsley, they go down real well!

Immature chicken mushroom

The mature specimen is another story. I don't know who started the rumor that these taste like chicken. In the mature specimen the shelves, when broken up, do have flesh that resembles the texture and color of cooked chicken breast. But that's where the resemblance ends. Sautéed, these might as well be cardboard. You may cut off some of the softer, actively growing shelf-ends and if you simmer them these may approximate the quality of the less mature form. You will find, at times, you will need to add water (or chicken stock). One can marinate the mature form (after boiling) and create an interesting side dish. Some very hard chickens, even after boiling for a half-hour, could still be very tough and not suitable for marinating. Once in a while a mature chicken has very soft shelves and may be quite good simmered. After 25 minutes or so you may add onions and stewed tomatoes followed in about five minutes by your egg batter. While consuming your omelet you may easily imagine that you are enjoying the chicken and the egg simultaneously!

There is a variant of this mushroom whose pores are white, instead of sulfur yellow, though the color of the upper sides is the same. Again, the younger the better. These should not be treated any differently than the yellow-pored chicken.

WINE-CAPS

Wine-caps

One day, my arborist friend George, who obviously has many opportunities to see a wide variety of fungi, brought some over for me to ID. After examining the physical characteristics, obtaining a spore print and looking at the spores under a microscope, I found that they were wine-caps, a delicious mushroom with a long growing season—May to November. Usually found in wood chips, they can achieve a large size, with fleshy caps as large as eight inches or more, reminiscent of portobellas. When young, their caps are burgundy in color, fading to tan with age. Their gills are nearly white to dusky when young and become a violet black with age. The stalks can also be ponderous. These "shrooms" are quite insect repellent and even the very large specimens are usually larvae-free. As with other stalked

Mature wine-caps

mushrooms, check for "worms" by examining the transected stalk at the base, which is where the larvae enter. If this is okay so is the rest of the mushroom.

But if there are any worms, serially cut the base towards the cap to try to get above the larvae and save the rest of the mushroom. Usually, one only eats the cap anyway because that's where the flavor is. By the way, should you miss a few larvae, fear not—you'll only ingest a little more protein!

Wine caps may grow in crops week after week in the same place. They grow rapidly and you'll see young and old ones in the same crop. Often it is not necessary to wash them, just wipe off the cap with a damp cloth and tap out any debris in the gills. The gills are often totally clear of foreign matter. Also, for a cleaner mushroom harvest, I would urge you to sever the stalk from its base and leave the latter behind, resisting the impulse to hastily remove the entire fruiting body from its environment. This temptation is strongest when one has come upon the mother-lode!

A similar mushroom, the garland Stropharia, grows on grass, thus often near wood chips and mulch; it doesn't grow as large as wine-caps and has a shorter stalk. Their caps are yellow to cream colored, even the young, with no trace of the burgundy color of the wine-caps. This Stropharia is thought to be poisonous. Knowing how the young specimen looks should alert one to this fungus. Clearly, for correct identification, it is important to recognize mushrooms at their different stages of maturity. Note, in the photos, how different the young and mature wine-caps. The young specimen has a burgundy colored, convex or dome-shaped cap and the gills are white. The mature wine-cap, on the other hand, has a cap which is more tan and flat and the gills are a deep purple. Furthermore, there are all the gradations in between. So things can get very complicated. Identification is made easier when the different stages of development are found together.

The mature forms of the wine-caps, with their deep purple gills, can be used to make a rich sauce for pasta.

Here's how Fortunata does it:

> Slice the fresh caps into strips, roughly 1 by 3 inches, and sauté with a small amount of extra virgin olive oil. The spores and water will be released into the pan, creating a rich brownish sauce.

> At the same time boil egg noodles (rice is great too!) until they are about half-done. Drain off most of the water, saving some in case needed.

> Add the wine-caps with their sauce to the noodles which, continuing to cook to *al dente*, absorb the flavor of the wine-caps. Top off with your favorite cheese. *Buon appetito*!

The young wine-caps with their thick bowl-shaped caps of various sizes are ideal for stuffing, using perhaps what you like in your turkey. I like to grill the large thick caps. Discard the stems, sprinkle liberally with the condiments you like and brush both sides with olive oil. With the grill on high, it'll take four to five minutes a side. You'll be surprised at the flavor! To me, these taste like a steak—without the calories! Wine-caps tend to grow in the same place the following year. I haven't had much luck finding them on new woodchips. Perhaps they have to break down a bit before they are a suitable substrate.

Most mushrooms are pretty bland, although I've read where this one tastes like lobster and that one smells like apricots. I believe it's more what you do with the mushroom to enhance the flavor that matters most. By the way, flavor equals taste, smell, texture and whatever other neurochemical circuits are activated in your brain! That being said, wine-caps, especially as a sauté for pasta or grilled, do produce their own unique flavor.

Here's one of Fortunata's recipes for stuffed wine-caps:

> Prepare caps. Wash with running water. You want the mushrooms moist for baking. Sprinkle with salt and garlic powder.
>
> In a bowl add 1 cup of chopped wine-caps (stems ok, if healthy), 1 cup of seasoned bread-crumbs, ¼ cup parmesan cheese, ¼ cup of fresh chopped parsley, ½ tsp. of black pepper, ¼ cup of extra virgin olive oil and ½ stick of melted butter. Mix thoroughly and stuff the caps!
>
> Place in baking dish to which has been added just enough water to cover the bottom. Top off each stuffed mushroom with a thin slice of cheese or butter, cover and bake at about 400° for 30 mins.

When one is lucky enough to find wine-caps in May, be sure to check that area at least weekly and all the way into November for new growth. Wine-caps grow rapidly so be sure to look for them a day or two after a good downpour. As is true of many mushrooms, they don't flourish during the summer months, but often come back strong in September. This is one of the most versatile and delicious of all the mushrooms that I have enjoyed. While the young wine-cap is great for stuffing, the mature specimen with its violet to nearly black gills are definitely more flavorful, an exception, in my opinion, to the greater desirability of the young mushroom. You won't find them in the woods. More likely you'll spot them, while driving around, in the woodchips on someone's property! So start looking when May arrives! A couple of points about obtaining mushrooms on private property: Ask permission! Usually, people are more than happy if you relieve them of their "toadstools"! Also, ask if they have treated the area with any chemicals.

Sumptuous Summer Finds

THE RUSSULA FAMILY

When I was a boy, our mushroom forays were pretty much limited to the fall season which usually meant honey mushrooms. My dad, however, would pick a variety of mushrooms, some of which my mother didn't trust, so she preserved these separately and they became known as "Jake's mushrooms." Many of these were gilled mushrooms, often a Russula or Lactarius species. For the most part these begin to appear during the summer months and continue growing into the fall. The Russula caps come in a variety of colors—red, green, purple, white, brown—and are terrestrial, as opposed to those that grow on trees, trunks, logs or buried wood. They have white gills and a thick brittle stalk which you can snap like chalk in your fingers. The flesh is also white. The most abundant cap color seems to be in the pink to red range, though these are also easier to spot. Avoid the bright red to scarlet cap which is slimy and has off-white or cream colored gills. This may be the emetic Russula, also known as "the sickener." You won't die, but you might wish you had!

Tom Volk, in his "Fungus of the Month" website of September, 2004, questioned whether the sickener really exists in North America but concludes that it probably does, "though its existence is probably restricted to sphagnum bogs." If you believe you have found one, taste a small piece. This is one time I make this recommendation, which I am usually loathe to do. If it has a hot peppery taste, you have found a Russula emetica. Don't swallow, just spit it out! I have eaten many red-capped Russulas and never have become ill, but no point tempting fate! I believe the Russulas are underrated as a culinary experience due to their abundance and their fragility.

As per David Arora,[14] some mushroomers would just as soon kick them as pick them. They shatter into a multitude of pieces! You even have to handle them gently lest they fragment. But

---

14 *Mushrooms Demystified* by Arora

here's how you deal with their fragility: After removing the stalks, soak the caps in warm salted water for a half hour or so. Then you will find that the caps will hold together and the salt will drive out any overlooked insect larvae. After this you can wash them in tap water—the cap surfaces are often covered with forest debris—and then boil them for five minutes. After draining in a colander, I like to blot up excess water with paper towels. Now they are ready for preparation.

Although the Russulae are terrestrial fungi, I have found them growing from deteriorated branches lying on the ground. One should not be fooled by this presentation.

Red-capped Russula

Variable Russula

Because of their anatomy and their fragility the Russulas are easy to identify as to genus. Species identification, however, can, in many cases, confound even the experts.

Note the multiple hues in the variable above, a good edible. Green, purple and pink are in these specimens. Another fine edible Russula is the beautiful green-quilt Russula shown below.

Green-quilt Russula

I enjoy fried Russulas. After treating them in the manner described above, I season them, coat with flour and fry them in extra virgin olive oil. What a treat! Instead of flour, you may prefer dipping in an egg batter and then bread crumbs. On washing mushrooms: You may read in different texts that you should not wash mushrooms. When I can avoid this, I do because mushrooms can really soak up the water. That said, I often find that it is better to wash them and then gently express the excess water. Do not wash or cut up your mushrooms until you are ready to prepare or preserve them. After hours in the woods, you might not feel like preparing your prizes. No need to work over them right away. If properly stored, they will keep in the fridge for several days. More on storing in the refrigerator later.

LATEX PRODUCING MUSHROOMS

The Lactarii also are terrestrials and belong, with the Russulae, to the Russulaceae[15] family. Like the Russulae, they also present with a variety of colors. They exude a sticky, milky latex from the gills and transected stalk. Thus the name Lactarius. They are not as brittle as the Russulae and they are more insect resistant. Perhaps the insects are not fond of the latex! They are also an excellent choice for frying as described above. In fact, any thin-capped mushroom can be fried. The firm white Lactarii don't fry up as well and are best marinated.

---

15 All family names end in "-aceae"

Also, avoid Lactarii whose sticky exudation is any color but white! Though there are exceptions, the beginner should stick to the white latex only specimens. Check the latex color on freshly picked Lactarii by cutting the gills near the stalk. If the white latex changes color, this mushroom should be avoided.

Corrugated cap milky

Hygrophorous milky

All of the Russulae and Lactarii are thought to be mycorrhizal. The brittleness of these mushrooms is due to the microscopic presence of large encysted cells forming structures known as sphaerocysts. However, it seems to me that the differences between the Russulae and the Lactarii are so great that I marvel that they are included in the same family. But I suppose that is true of any family!

Fortunata introduced me to the pleasures of eating fried mushrooms so I now enjoy eating "Jake's mushrooms"! My dad had his own nomenclature for the Russulae and the Lactarii. To him, who was not acquainted with the word terrestrial, they were all "field mushrooms," growing directly out of the ground. Mycophiles throughout the world have long had their own way of referring to their favorites. Maybe not taxonomically correct, but certainly not affecting the gastronomic experience!

Voluminous latex milky

Jake would sometimes bring home a chicken mushroom or a hen of the woods. He would call these *signorinas* but to my mother they were still "Jake's mushrooms" and would be preserved, separately, for him. One of his *signorinas*[16] weighed in at 79 pounds and was featured in the local papers. By the way, in case you're wondering, Jake lived into his 90s! So the point is, I suppose, that sometimes "Father knows best"!

CHANTERELLES

The next group of mushrooms all belong to the Chantharellaceae family and make their appearance in the summer months, most abundantly in July. These include the chanterelle, the smooth chanterelle, the red chanterelle and the black trumpet, among others. These are all great edible mushrooms that lack true gills and can often be found in abundance, frequently in the same location year after year. So it helps to remember your mushroom spots. The reason mushrooms tend to grow again in the same location is due to the persistence of the hidden vegetative portion which may survive from year to year, as long as there is enough organic substrate from which it can obtain its nourishment.

16 *Signorina* = Italian for young woman

The chanterelle

The chanterelle is perhaps the most desired of the four, but what's to account for taste? They are yellow and their pseudo-gills are well-defined. They are said to smell like apricots. Having eaten many apricots right off the tree, I tried but could not detect the bouquet, so I asked Fortunata, holding some under her nose, "Do these smell like apricots?" And she said "Sure!" So I made an appointment with a nose specialist! The caps get up to about three inches and, when mature, are broadly vase-shaped as are all these mushrooms.

Smooth chanterelles

You should not confuse the chanterelle, or the smooth chanterelle, with the poisonous jack-o-lantern. (page 32). The latter grows on wood, often in large clumps, has a more intense orange color and can be much larger than any of the chanterelles.

The smooth chanterelle, also yellow but paler, is so-called because the

Washing red and smooth chanterelles

pseudo-gills appear melted down and blend into each other, as you can see in the picture. These are firmer than the chanterelle, about the same size or slightly larger and seem more insect repellent.

Red chanterelles are a bit smaller at maturity than the previous two. Even two-inch caps are not very common so you have to work harder to get a meal. These are quite firm, especially the stalks, and are also quite insect resistant. Like the chanterelle their pseudo-gills, which are really ridges or folds, are well-defined and with a cursory glance one might think they were gills like other mushrooms have. Because of their size and tendency to clump, it's perhaps easier to harvest them with a scissors, leaving the base of the stalk in the soil. They have a peppery taste and, it is said, can be eaten raw, an apparent exception

Red chanterelles

23

to the rule—do not eat wild mushrooms that are not cooked. I have, in fact, eaten a few raw and appreciated their piquancy, but like all mushrooms their digestibility improves when cooked!

They often grow slowly, over several weeks, before they are large enough to pick. They are a colorful addition to salads. The chanterelle, smooth chanterelle and red chanterelle retain their firmness even after washing, so don't hesitate to do so.

Black trumpets, though not a chanterelle genus, belong to the same family. These hollow mushrooms, whose color varies from gray to brown to black, depending on climatic and soil conditions, resemble the end of a trumpet and are the most vase-like. Their size is comparable to the chanterelle and the smooth chanterelle, but their margins are less wavy. These fungi have a rich earthy flavor and are a welcome addition to many recipes. I like them in omelets! Their strong flavor would overpower that of many other mushrooms and, in my opinion, are best not combined with them. Since there is virtually no flesh in these, there is no larval infestation although mature critters may lie within the trumpet cavity. I would prefer not to wash these because, since they are hollow, they will collapse into an unattractive amorphous, black mass. However, their wonderful flavor is not affected, so wash if you must. Drying is the preferred method of preservation by many.

Black trumpets

The horn of plenty, which looks like the black trumpet, has a white spore print while the black trumpet has an ochre-buff to orange print. No matter, the horn of plenty is also very desirable.

All of these mushrooms can be found alongside unpaved forest roads, often growing in moss or among ferns, old leaves and other low plant growth. Because of their color, the trumpets can be easily overlooked. Cut off the stalks of the first three and just the part that was underground of the trumpets. Then wash them in cold water. It usually takes three or four rinses to clean them. Because the chanterelles are often found alongside dirt roads, they tend to be sandy—but the sand rinses off easily. After draining and compressing slightly to get rid of excess water (they don't absorb much), they can be sautéed and eaten right away or frozen for later use. I usually combine onions with mushrooms. They are made for each other, like peas and carrots! Trumpets, sautéed with a small amount of olive oil, can be used to create a pasta sauce in the manner described for wine-caps, but layer the sautéed trumpets with their sauce over *fully-cooked* pasta of your choice, topped with your favorite cheese.

Casseroles often contain an interesting medley of ingredients and so would welcome the inclusion of a hearty mushroom, such as the trumpet or the mature wine-cap, in a dish where the flavor of a more subtle-tasting fungus would be lost.

BOLETES

The boletes belong to the Boletaceae family and include several hundred species, all characterized by pores on the undersurface of the cap, instead of gills. The pores are the openings into tubes, where the spores are located. These are found in the summer and fall and include many edible species, the most prized of which is the King Bolete, commonly referred to as porcini or cep. My experience has been that the porcini are most abundant during July. The color of the cap surface is quite variable and can be light brown to cinnamon or dark brown and even reddish brown. It has thick white flesh overlying a thick pore layer. The stalk [stipes] is also quite thick and may be decidedly enlarged toward the base. The white to light brown stalk has a delicate lacy network especially on its upper third. The thick brown cap reminds one of buns, though the pore layer is whitish, when young, becoming yellow-brown with age. The pores may bruise a tawny color, but not blue.

Almost all boletes are mycorrhizal, enjoying their symbiotic underground connections with trees and bushes. These choice fungi are prepared in many ways, sautéed, etc. The large caps are excellent grilled, like the wine-caps. They can be stored frozen but should be cooked first. This can be accomplished in a variety of ways: sautéing in butter or oil, blanched, steamed, etc. They will keep for several months. Uncooked mushrooms don't do well when frozen. They get too mushy. Like other mushrooms they can be stored in the refrigerator for a few days as long as there is adequate circulation of air without which condensation would cause them to become slimy. I like to use a colander for this purpose although many people use paper bags because of their porosity. *Cook's Illustrated* magazine of September–October 2008 says a partially unzipped plastic bag also works. Ideally mushrooms are best consumed shortly after harvesting. Nothing beats eating fresh mushrooms.

Porcini

Many people dry porcini. This concentrates the aroma and flavor and when reconstituted in water are a tasty addition to many recipes. Several years ago I ran into an old-timer, George, who was accustomed to drying his boletes and I got a whiff of his dried bicolors that had been sitting in this large jar for years. What a strong fragrance!

He and his wife, both in their 80's, were still using these to flavor their recipes. He had dried these in the sun for two days. Didn't need any special equipment! You might prefer to purchase a food dehydrator, or simply dry them in your oven.

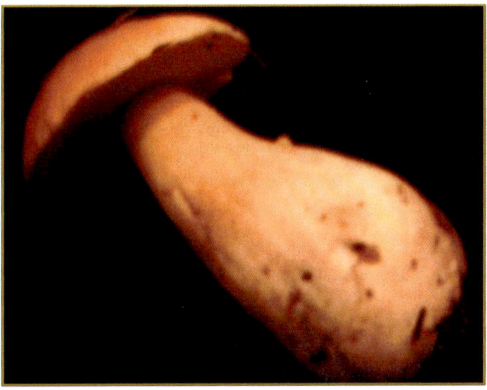

A young porcino

Instead of using water to reconstitute, you can jazz up your porcini by reconstituting with wine or, perhaps, warm cream. The thick, fleshy caps of many boletes are ideal for drying. If the pore layer is too mushy, just peel this layer off and discard, thus salvaging the abundant flesh. When reconstituted, you may find the flavor to be intensified. Some years these terrestrial mushrooms can be found in great numbers, but the crop is variable and depends largely on climatic conditions, as does the crop of all mushrooms! In Connecticut the 2007 drought affected both the summer and fall mushrooms very badly. Although there were some finds, the harvest that year was the worst in a long time. In '05 the summer mushroom crop was devastated by the drought and the autumn fungi were hurt by the excessive rainfall. In '04, both summer and fall mushrooms were present in healthy abundance. The porcini crop was the best in a long time and we found and consumed plenty! Porcini are found under both conifers and deciduous trees. As I am writing this, in early August of '08, many boletes, as well as mushrooms of other families, are present in abundance, thanks to the most abundant rainfall in years. When you are so blessed, take advantage of your opportunities and get out there as often as you can!

There are many mushrooms which closely resemble porcini though it is not clear if they are merely variants or actually represent different species. Perhaps both explanations will be found to be true. DNA studies may shed some light on this complex of mushrooms or, it is possible, may create further confusion. I, for one, will not allow any such haggling to interfere with my enjoyment of this wonderful fungus.

Many of the boletes will stain various colors when handled—blue, green, brown, red, yellow, purple and black. This is referred to as "bruising" and may occur even though the specimen is carefully handled. Blue-staining boletes, although some are good edibles, should be avoided by the beginner because some will make you ill, mainly gastrointestinal disturbances. Also, don't eat any bolete whose pores are red or orange for the same reason.

Now that I've recommended that you avoid all blue-staining boletes, I shall relate to you the desirability of finding and enjoying the bicolored bolete, which has a wine-red to rose colored cap, tiny yellow pores and a stalk which is mostly rose-red colored. All parts, except the flesh of the stalk slowly bruising blue. The yellow flesh of the stalk may bruise blue slowly, if at all.

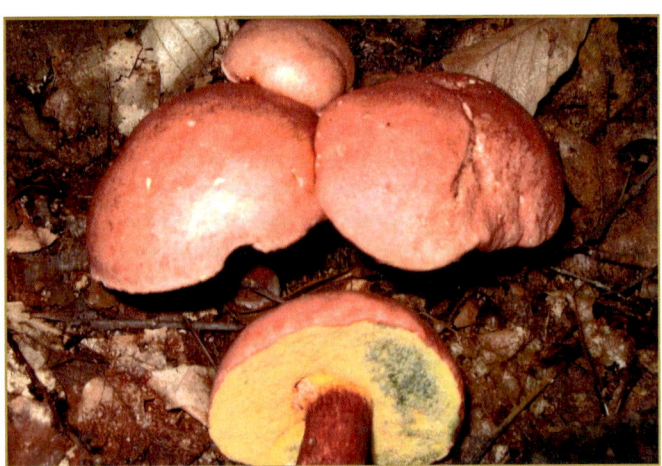

Two-colored bolete

This choice edible can be often be found in July, in the same environs and at the same time as porcinis. It may also be found in September until early fall. It must be distinguished from the brick cap bolete whose parts *all* bruise blue instantly. Its stalk is mostly yellow

Young bicolors

and its flesh also bruises deep blue rapidly. This causes gastrointestinal distress and should be avoided. I know mushroomers who have consumed both bicolor and brick cap boletes for years with no ill effect! In Calabria, Italy, they boil these fungi to leech out most of the blue color and then keep them in the fridge in cold water, changing the water until clear. They are then ready for preparation. Perhaps this rids the brick cap of its toxic quality, but I still avoid this mushroom. Furthermore, the leeching process renders the specimens entirely too mushy.

Common scaber stalks

The common scaber stalk, though not a bolete, is along with boletes a member of the Boletaceae family. It is often found in great abundance during the summer and fall. Their stalks feature black projections, the scabers. Easy to identify, their succulent caps make them an excellent culinary choice.

When cleaning boletes, the pore layer at times may be found to be too water-laden or insect damaged or infested. If the flesh is good, just discard the pore layer. It's easy to spot larval infestation in the bicolor because its yellow flesh turns brown along the paths of the larvae.

There are many fine edible boletes. The book by Bessette, Roody and Bessette[17] is an excellent guide to identifying boletes. Several hundred Boletus species are described here with excellent photos. Books will only take you so far. In addition, you must go with an experienced mushroomer, who will examine *each and every* mushroom that you pick!

---

17 *North American Boletes*, First Edition, 2000

The Pause That Refreshes

Although an unusually wet August may extend the growing season for summer mushrooms, by mid-month this season is essentially over, the hot summer weather having taken its toll. But you may find a few red chanterelles, perhaps some Lactarii, a chicken mushroom or some oysters. You might be tempted to pick a black-staining polypore. Although considered, by some, a good edible when young, I'm not a fan. They can achieve impressive size but are barely edible. Too stringy! The mature specimen is not even salvageable by marinating. I've tried! This one was three feet by one and a half feet, growing from an oak stump. The black staining on its upper portion is due to lawn work. Perhaps a less mature specimen would have been more palatable!

Black-staining polypore

You might also see a large cluster of bright orange mushrooms with orange gills, the beautiful but poisonous jack-o-lantern. Don't confuse these with chanterelles! It should be difficult to confuse the jack-o-lantern with the chanterelle. The jack-o-lantern is generally larger, with a larger cap and thicker stalk, very orange and grows on wood in large clumps. In the pictures on this page, those at upper left are relatively young. In the mature specimen, below on the right, the caps can appear more vase-like as the edges evert and the cap center becomes depressed. Still, there have been errors in identification. Bide your time. Better days are coming! Good finds are few and far between from mid-August to early September. I like to think of this time as "between seasons"—too late for summer mushrooms but too early for fall ones.

Young jack-o-lanterns

Mature jack-o-lanterns

As September cools and the days are noticeably shorter, but more pleasant, we see a resurgence of some of the spring and summer mushrooms. Wine-caps often return as well as Russulae, Lactarii, red chanterelles, black trumpets and various boletes. But don't expect to see morels. You'll have to wait until next spring for these. Honey mushrooms make their appearance in early September and will continue to grow, often in great abundance, until late October. The ring-less honey mushroom may appear earlier, but they are not as desirable. If I can't resist picking these, it's because I want to add their caps to a stew of whatever venison is left from the previous fall!

Autumn Adventures

One late September afternoon my friend George called me and, in excited tones, told me of this large cluster of mushrooms that he found on a stump. "I think they're honey mushrooms!" After he described them, I said "I don't think so. Better bring them over." Well, there must have been a hundred of them, all in one large cluster and they did resemble honey mushrooms but their color had an orange cast and the gills were similarly colored. The spore print was rust orange, so I knew they were not honeys, whose spore print is white. After a little more research and checking the spores microscopically, I realized that this attractive cluster was a big laughing gym, an hallucinogenic mushroom that causes uncontrollable laughter and inappropriate behavior. After very brief consideration, I decided not to experiment, but instead, I took to heart the words of an old sage: "There's no fool like an old fool!"

Big laughing gym

HONEY MUSHROOMS

Honey mushrooms make their appearance in early September and will continue to grow, crop-like, until late October. It's been said that you cannot find a single honey mushroom and they often grow in great abundance. Edibility-wise the honey is variously rated from good to choice. Most commonly these have yellow or brown caps with whitish gills and a ring on the upper stalk which is usually fairly thick and white to yellow or brown. The yellow honey is often firmer with large thick button-like caps. The early appearing and lighter brown specimen seems more perishable and may present with a strain that has thin caps and stalks. The late September and October brown honeys are a darker brown with thicker caps and stalks. Look for these on stumps or buried wood especially of oak trees. In fact, they are so commonly, though not exclusively, associated with oaks that my dad used to call them "oaks." It was years before I learned their real name, but a rose by any other name, etc. Honey mushrooms grow rapidly, as do many mushrooms, and are quite perishable. I like to look for them no later than 1-2 days after a steady rain. Too much rain will waterlog them; if it's too dry, they are subject to insect infestation.

Young honey mushrooms

Usually they are not found on the stumps of newly cut trees or on very old deteriorated ones. It seems that the new stumps haven't deteriorated enough and the very old crumbly ones have had all the nutrients leeched from them and so are not suitable for this parasitic and saprophytic fungus. The honey mushroom is held in low regard in some quarters because of its ability to attack and destroy certain otherwise healthy plants, bushes and trees. So, like Rodney Dangerfield, they don't get any respect! I also believe the honey is underrated because it can often be found in such abundance. It's not unusual to find hundreds of honeys on a stump.

Mature, brown honey mushroom caps

The young, in the button form, are often marinated. I like these in omelets, with onions of course, and whatever else suits your palate. In the cap form they are a good addition to stews, especially venison stews. In fact, wild mushrooms and game food are a marriage made in heaven. If you fry the caps, gently express the excess water before seasoning, dipping in flour and frying in extra virgin olive oil. The stalks of the older honeys, both yellow and brown, can be quite woody so don't eat these unless you have the patience to shave off the bark-like outer layer! My mother liked to sauté honeys with olive oil, garlic, oregano and pieces of hot Italian sausage. A meal in itself! But, perhaps overkill for the nuanced palate!

When young, honey mushroom caps are often button-shaped, as are the young of many mushrooms. The cap flattens some as the honey matures, though a central boss (bump) may persist. The button shape, along with a partial veil, serves to protect the developing spores. Some honeys, even when large, retain their youthful appearance and, with a thick stalk, really look phallic! This seems to occur more with the yellow honeys. The caps have fine "hairs" which project from the surface. These are readily seen in the picture on page 37 showing the mature caps. The photo also shows a white, powder-like deposits on two of the caps which are spores that have dropped from overlying gills.

Young yellow honeys

After cleaning and boiling these for several minutes, they may be put in freezer bags and they will keep a long time in your freezer. My mother used to boil for five minutes, drain, express excess water and pack with a lot of salt into Mason jars. They stay good indefinitely but be sure to rinse off the salt before preparing. Once I sautéed a bunch of these, forgetting to rinse off the salt. What a disappointment and waste of perfectly fine mushrooms!

The attractive golden pholiota grows, often in impressive clumps, in the same environs as the honey mushroom. Said to be edible, it closely resembles other species which can cause gastrointestinal disturbances. It should therefore be avoided. The large scales on the cap in contrast to the fine hairs of the honey can distinguish the two. Also, its spore print is brown.

Golden pholiota

The deadly Galerina, a little brown mushroom or LBM, is smaller than the honey and has a thin stalk and a rusty brown spore print so it is not hard to distinguish it from the honey mushroom. Its toxin is the same as the destroying angel and the death cap! Since this also grows on wood, you need to beware of it. In general, avoid all LBMs.

THE HEN OF THE WOODS

The hen of the woods, an autumn mushroom, is found in September and October, usually at the base of deciduous trees, especially oaks and on their stumps. Like the chicken mushroom, the hen is also a stalked polypore, but has a very different appearance, with gray, brown or even whitish-gray spoon shaped petals and white flesh. Also, like the chicken mushroom, the hen can achieve a great size, but unlike the chicken even large mature specimens are magnificent edibles. In my opinion this is the best of the fall season finds. One often will see this wonderful fungus while driving along suburban residential roads where there are many oak trees. They are often overlooked because of their indistinct coloration. At first glance, they might be passed off as a clump of fallen leaves. So drive slowly, especially from mid-September to well into October and check out the bases of the larger oak trees, which they prefer over smaller ones.

It's not unusual to find more than one, so be sure to look all around the tree base. There were five hens on the base of the oak tree shown below.

Fortunata with hens of the woods

When found close to the road, sand, kicked up by passing cars can imbed in the growing hen and render it virtually inedible, unless one enjoys the grittiness! You then can scrape off the individual petals but this is labor intensive and not particularly rewarding. When found a few feet above the road or away from it, there is little, if any sand. The hen is also quite insect resistant, except for mature critters which you expel when you cut it up.

In Japan, where this also grows, the hen is known as maitake. It is said to have medicinal, even anti-cancer properties. While there are many claims for the therapeutic properties of fungi, many are anecdotal. Legitimate research has led to important discoveries, and, no doubt, will find many more. Remember penicillin? Discovered in 1928 by Fleming, this mold-derived antibiotic has saved countless lives! The cyclosporins, antibiotics derived from fungal fermentation, were a boon for the field of organ transplantation when they were found to be effective in preventing organ rejection.

Hen of the woods (and the author)

I find the name interesting. It doesn't look like a hen and most of the ones I've found were in suburbia, not in the woods! Maybe a name change is in order?

After cutting and cleaning, I boil for about ten minutes, depending on how firm they are, and store in freezer bags. They can be simmered with a variety of delectable, complementary veggies and interesting sauces.

After they are defrosted, be sure to gently express excess water. The pores will absorb whatever sauce suits your fancy, and this is the magical quality of the hen! Don't try to get all the water out! Some mushroom moisture is important to combine with your sauce.

Here is a delicious penne/hen recipe alla Fortunata:

> Sauté onions in extra virgin olive oil and add in the hen when the onions are translucent. Crush one can of stewed tomatoes over the hen. Season to taste.
>
> You may add some marinara sauce—tomato with basil—if desired.
>
> Simmer for about 45 minutes. The pores will soak up the flavor! Spoon this over penne or the pasta of your choice, cooked *al dente*. You'll love it!

Since they are a firm mushroom, they are also a good candidate for marinating. Also, some dry, very firm hens may be salvaged by marinating, though they are not suitable for other dishes.

Hen of the woods

The predominately white hen above was found in a very dark forest, mostly hemlock, that French-Indian hunting guides refer to as "the dark wood" because so little light gets in. I believe this accounts for its lack of coloration. It's likely that we would have missed it altogether if it were brown.

The 2008 season for "hen-hunting" was very rewarding. It seemed there were hens everywhere, both at the usual locations and in many new areas which, you can be sure, we visited again in 2009 though, regretfully, with less success.

BRICK TOPS

Brick tops

Perhaps the most persistent of the good edible fall mushrooms are the brick tops,[18] also members of the Strophariaceae family, which grow from September through November, and are so called because of their brick-colored caps, the color fading toward yellow near the edge. The gills are dusky, when young, becoming violet with age. My dad used to call these "chestnuts" because of their attractive color. The caps are usually no larger than 1½ to somewhat less than 4 inches in diameter. As with most fungi, the younger ones are preferred. I've always enjoyed their pleasant aroma when first coming upon them. They may be found in large clusters on stumps, logs and wood chips. Their appearance has always signaled to me that the year's mushroom

---

18 This is a gilled mushroom. Don't confuse with the brick-cap bolete.

season is drawing to a close, and somehow this fills me with melancholy nostalgia.

I've even picked them in early December and the cold late autumn nights help to spare them from larval infestation. Don't confuse these with the poisonous sulfur tuft. Difficult to do for the latter have yellow caps.

I like to cut away the stems, wash if necessary, again expressing excess water, and fry or saute' them with butter and onions and, perhaps, mix them into an omelet, and relive the highlights of the season's fungal forays.

Other Delectable Goodies

With the exception of morels, which can be difficult to find, I have been fortunate indeed to have harvested and enjoyed all of the fine mushrooms in this presentation in great abundance. Let me assure you, however, that there are many other fine edibles in New England. All of the mushrooms, already discussed and those about to be presented, grow in other locales, although there are, to be sure, regional differences. Many are also popular in European countries and in other places where climatic conditions are similar to here. The edibility of some mushrooms is unknown and the identity of others is yet to be established. The mushroom story is a never ending saga!

MUSHROOMS WITH TEETH

There are some fine delectables which I have found and enjoyed, but, unfortunately, not in large amounts. This is not to say that these mushrooms cannot be found in large quantities, only that I haven't been so lucky. Two of these are fungi that have neither gills nor pores, but bear their spores on teeth or spines. Aside from this shared peculiarity, they don't resemble each other in the least. The first, sweet

Sweet tooth

tooth or hedgehog mushroom, is easily recognized by its orange cap with in-rolled and/or wavy margin, overlying short pointed yellow to pale orange spines and a thick stalk. This firm mushroom is rather insect resistant and has a pleasant flavor. A terrestrial, it grows under conifers and deciduous trees during the summer and fall.

The bear's head grows from summer to fall on old deciduous stumps, logs and the wounds of trees, especially maple. While the teeth are fragile—though edible—the flesh is highly desirable. It may be my imagination but the abundant, compact, pure white flesh, sliced one quarter to a half-inch and simmered, tastes like the flesh of a delicate Nova Scotia lobster! You might prefer to slice real thin and fry or sauté this prize. There are several related species, all choice edibles, particularly when young, and there are no poisonous look-alikes. This specimen was about 15 feet up the trunk. Using a long pole, my young friend George was able to dislodge it and I made a "perfect reception"!

Bear's head tooth high on the tree trunk

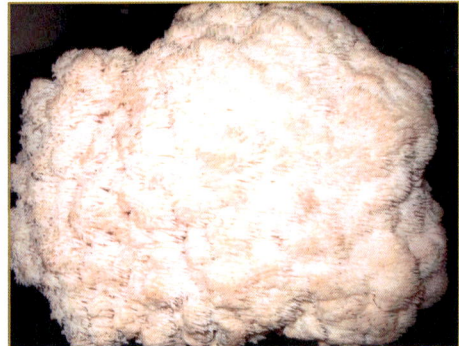

Bear's head tooth

FRIED CHICKEN, ANYONE?

The fried chicken mushroom tends to grow in large clusters in grassy areas alongside paths and roads and also near old sawdust piles and waste areas. The firm caps are gray-brown and the thick, white stalks do not have a ring. The spore print is white. This is another mushroom said to taste like *chicken*! Don't know where some people get their ideas! Anyway this is a good edible and because of their abundance and firmness, you can do a lot with them. If the caps are not too large, I'd be inclined to marinate them. Another plus is they seem insect resistant. These are found in the summer and fall.

Fried chicken mushroom

OR WOULD YOU PREFER A NICE STEAK?

The beefsteak mushroom grows on trees, dead or alive, and on stumps and logs of deciduous trees, usually oaks. Its name derives from the fact that it looks like a piece of liver. This polypore has a thick, slimy, reddish cap which is often tongue-shaped and amongst Italian mushroom aficionados it is known as *lingua*, which means tongue and I do believe this mushroom more closely resembles a tongue than a piece of liver! Its pores vary from white, when young, to yellow and to reddish brown. The cut surface appears marbled and oozes a pink to red fluid, which makes it look like beef. I prefer to marinate this mushroom. Unfortunately, I have missed several opportunities to photograph this most peculiar fungus. Once you have seen it, it can hardly be confused with any other mushroom.

RED-CAPPED SCABER STALK

The strikingly beautiful red-capped scaber stalk is a magnificent find. Related to the common scaber stalk, this member of the Boletaceae family can grow thick fleshy caps, up to 8" in diameter. They are a good candidate for grilling. Even large caps are often larvae free. The cap color is more orange than red, as shown below. You will find these from mid-summer well into the fall and there are no poisonous look-alikes to my knowledge.

A fleshy find—Red-capped scaber stalk

The Bonus

Mother: Why don't you eat your spinach, Johnny?

Johnny: I don't like it!

Mother: How do you know if you haven't tried it? (Reasonable, but reason rarely works when it's up against preconception or delusion. It has to simmer for a while, maybe a long while, before it has a chance of succeeding.)

Father: Eat it; it's good for you. It has lots of iron. It'll make you strong, like Popeye! (Now Johnny is thinking: 'It'll probably make me look like him too, with his weird arms and his equally weird looking girlfriend, Olive Oyl!' He reluctantly tries a miniscule piece, makes a disgusting face to show his absolute revulsion and his parents back off.)

When I first began to look for mushrooms, it was because I wanted to share an adventure with my dad. It was like looking for lost treasure. Then I found that I enjoyed eating them because they tasted good, especially the way my mother prepared them! As time went on, I found that I loved every aspect of the mushroom experience, from finding them to preparing, eating or preserving them! I also enjoyed identifying new (to me) delectables which I could bring to the table. And it was all because of my dad whose enthusiasm for these fungi had such an impact on me! He never once said I should eat them because they "were good for" me. If he had, I might not have liked them at all.

That said, I have to also say that mushrooms *are* good for you! They are low in calories, salt and carbohydrates. They contain almost no fat and no cholesterol at all. Mushrooms contain a higher percentage of protein than most plants and not much less than meats. Also, they are rich in the vitamin B complex, especially riboflavin, niacin and pantothenic acid. Significant amounts of copper, potassium, selenium and phosphorous are present. Iron, zinc, manganese and magnesium are also present. Dietary fiber is present in healthy amounts.

The US Department of Agriculture National Nutrient Database for Standard Reference, which is readily available on the internet, reports on the nutrient content of a variety of mushrooms (and many other foodstuffs) both cooked and uncooked. These reports are updated on a regular basis.

The medicinal qualities of mushrooms have been emphasized by Asian countries, most notably China and Japan, for centuries. Although many of the claims are anecdotal, there is a growing body of evidence relating mushroom consumption to health.

Mushrooms are one of the largest sources of antioxidants, particularly polyphenols and ergothioneine, the latter being one of the most powerful antioxidants known. As a result of metabolic processes, our bodies form what are known as "free radicals." These are atoms with unpaired electrons and are highly reactive, leading to chain reactions as they try to pair up their electrons; this can lead to cellular damage, including damage to DNA.

This process then can lead to chronic diseases, including cancer and atherosclerosis among other unhealthy effects. Antioxidants stop this process by interrupting the chain reaction. I know, more than you need to know, perhaps! But humor me! Although our bodies have their own antioxidant system, it is overwhelmed at times; moreover, it grows less efficient with age. So there is a need to obtain additional antioxidants from other sources. And there are many foods which contain antioxidants, but mushrooms are perhaps the best source. I'm not going to tell you to eat your mushrooms, but you should know that some nutritionists are referring to them as a "superfood"!

About Poisonous Mushrooms

DEADLY MUSHROOMS

While you are looking for the many the many varieties of colorful and edible summer mushrooms you will no doubt come across a very pretty, all-white, but deadly mushroom, the destroying angel. The consumption of one of these can lead to death due to kidney and/or liver failure! Because of this I would advise all novices to avoid all totally white mushrooms. Transplant surgery has salvaged some lives but the mortality rate is still frightfully high. The destroying angel is also common in the fall, when another deadly mushroom, the death-cap, makes its appearance. The anatomy of the death cap is similar to the destroying angel—with the skirt-like ring and the membranous cup (volva) around the base—but its cap has a metallic greenish hue. These two mushrooms are responsible for most of the fatal mushroom poisonings, due to the toxin alpha amantine. Both also belong to the Amanitaceae family.

Destroying angels, mature on the left, and immature, above

Be sure to check the base of the stalk; it is surrounded by a cup-like structure, the volva. This is a remnant of the universal veil. The annulus is often extended as a skirt-like structure. Both of these Amanitas have a white spore print as do all of the mushrooms of the Amanitaceae family.

The deadly Galerina, an autumn (and spring) mushroom contains the same toxin as the destroying angel and the death cap. This and the deadly Cort are two little brown mushrooms—"LBMs"—that must be avoided. The message, worth repeating, is avoid all LBMs!

Another Amanita species, the fly agaric,[19] also makes its appearance during the summer months and into the fall. It is often depicted in stories of fantasy and magic, especially in children's books. This is that strikingly pretty red (or yellow) capped mushroom with the white flecks on the cap surface.

Yellow fly agaric

While not deadly, this causes delirium, raving and profuse sweating. Its Siberian equivalent is an hallucinogenic fungus, experimented with for centuries; it has even been regarded by some as divine. Its ef-

---

19 Agaric = a term applied to any mushroom with gills on the underside of its cap

fects include euphoria, auditory and/or visual hallucinations, increased vigor and stamina and enhanced personality attributes, whether desirable or undesirable! Certainly a beautiful mushroom to see but I cannot recommend its consumption for recreational purposes! In the east the yellow fly agaric is more common. What looks like milk curds on the cap are the cottony remnants of the universal veil which surrounds the entire early developing fruiting body. On page 52 they are shown in the button stage. The novice should avoid all mushrooms that have caps with these curd-like veil remnants on them.

※

There are many other poisonous mushrooms and others that are considered possibly poisonous. Some of these can be confused with good edibles so you will need to be able to distinguish the desirable mushrooms from the poisonous look-alikes. Simply put, any fungus labeled "poisonous" must be avoided. The toxic reaction can be mild or deadly! Take no chances! A mushroom that is "probably okay to eat" is no good at all! NO EXCEPTIONS.

Often, when someone is said to have suffered from mushroom poisoning, it means something other than having consumed a poisonous fungus. Overindulgence is a common cause of gastrointestinal disturbances due to the indigestibility of the chitin in the mushroom cell wall. This nitrogen containing polysaccharide is reduced by cooking but not eliminated. Thoroughly cook your mushrooms. If you drink alcohol, limit your intake! Mushrooms and alcohol don't mix well!

Should you touch a poisonous mushroom, fear not! It will do you no harm. Also, as when consuming any new food, eat a small portion at first. Some people have idiosyncratic reactions. Although it has been suggested by many experts, I do *not* taste a small piece of a mushroom to see if it is edible!

There persist "techniques" which are used to tell if a mushroom is poisonous. Some place a silver spoon or coin amid the cooking mushrooms and if it tarnishes, the mushrooms are thought to be poisonous. Others use a clove of garlic and if it turns black the mushroom is not safe to eat! These tests are not reliable and should not be used. The only safeguard is correct identification! It's not unusual, after all efforts have been made—examining the specimen, looking at pictures, using identification keys in various texts—to be unable to ID the mushroom. Even the experts can't ID every specimen! Well, you know what to do: throw it out!

Practical Considerations

It's easy to get turned around in the woods, become disorientated and then realize that you are lost! This is especially true when you are on relatively flat land on cloudy days. In these circumstances, neither the topography nor the location of the sun are helpful, so it's a good idea to carry a compass! If you know the direction you entered, you will know the way out. Trust your compass! If you forgot your compass, you can use your watch to orient yourself. Point the hour-hand at the sun; half-way between that and 12 on your watch is due south (in the Northern Hemisphere).

If allergic, keep an eye out for poison ivy or other vegetation you are sensitive to. In the moist warm woods, mosquitoes and no-see-ums can be a problem, especially during the summer months. So wear long sleeves and have insect repellent handy. Tucked-in trousers, boots and cap provide additional protection.

Also beware of deer ticks, which may carry the bacterium[20] that causes Lyme disease. Insect sprays containing 20-30% DEET[21] afford effective protection against these ticks. When you get home, be sure to check your body and clothing for deer ticks.

In some parts of Connecticut there are timber rattlers, notably in Meshomasic State Forest. So wear boots and look where you are walking. Some mushroomers like to use a walking stick. The timber rattler, a protected species, is venomous, but fortunately not aggressive. I like to slowly cruise the dirt roads in the state forest. You can cover a lot of woods this way and see many desirable mushrooms growing near the roadside, and, with a little experience, get a good idea of what's growing and where and when it might be opportune to do a little walking. One day, while slowly driving in the forest, I spotted a three-foot timber rattler, at the edge of the road, about eight feet from my SUV. It was stretched out, parallel to the road in a shady, moist area and not coiled up in the warm sun on a rock, which would seem more likely.

---

20 The spirochete, *Borrelia burgdorferi*
21 DEET-diethyltoluamide. 'Cutter Outdoorsman' insect repellent contains 30% DEET

I stopped and studied the snake, noting its diamond shaped head, rattle and black-barred body. After a minute or so, it got tired of being so examined and slithered away. I chose not to see where it was headed. It is said that this reptile will not strike unless provoked, so, in the unlikely event that you come upon one, just walk away slowly. Surely, it's a good idea to know what creatures might inhabit the woods you choose to enter!

Bring a pocket knife, so you can harvest your mushrooms by cutting across the stalks, thus leaving dirt and/or organic debris behind. Most assuredly, this will simplify the cleaning process! I would urge you also to keep different specimens separate from each other, because, often, they will be preserved or prepared separately. Most definitely, mushrooms which need to be identified must be kept separate from the others! Collection baskets should be well-ventilated, so your finds stay fresh.

Don't forget your camera! With digital cameras it's easy for anyone to get quality close-ups with high resolution. A small one will slip right into your pocket, freeing your hands for other activity.

Glossary

Agaric – a mushroom with gills on the underside of its cap.

Annulus – a ring or collar of tissue on the stalk, the remnant of the partial veil.

Bolete – a fleshy mushroom of the Boletaceae family which has pores on the underside of its cap rather than gills.

Bruising – mushrooms which change color when handled.

Button – the immature stage of a mushroom, before its cap opens. It may appear to be dome or button-shaped.

Cap – the top or head of a mushroom.

Chitin – the main component of the fungal cell wall. It reduces digestibility.

Conifer – a cone-bearing tree.

Cup – the sac-like tissue at the base of some mushrooms. See volva.

Deciduous tree – one that sheds its leaves annually, such as the oak or maple.

Family – a group of related genera.

Flesh – the interior tissue of a mushroom.

Fruiting body – the reproductive portion of a fungus, which usually appears above the ground.

Fungus – an organism that lacks chlorophyll and possesses spores.

Genus – a group of related species.

Gill – one of the fleshy, blade-like plates that radiate from the stem, on the underside of the cap, to the cap margin. Also called lamellae.

Habitat – natural place of growth.

Hypha – a microscopic, thread-like structure, the basic cellular unit of any mushroom.

Lignin – an organic substance which, along with cellulose, makes up the major part of wood.

Margin – the outer edge of a mushroom cap.

Microscopic – visible only with a microscope.

Mushroom – the fruiting body of a fungus.

Mycelium – a mass of hyphae, typically hidden in a substrate.

Mycology – the study of fungi.

Mycorrhiza – a symbiotic association between a fungus and the rootlets of a plant or tree.

Parasitic – feeding on a living plant or animal.

Partial veil – a tissue which covers and protects the immature spore-bearing area—gills or tubes—of some mushrooms.

Polypore – any of a large group of firm, wood inhabiting fungi which bear their spores in pores.

Pore – the opening or mouth of the tube in boletes and polypores through which spores leave the mushroom.

Photosynthesis – the manufacture of complex organic compounds such as glucose, a simple carbohydrate, from water, carbon dioxide and sunlight, with the aid of chlorophyll. Plants do this; mushrooms cannot.

Ring – see annulus.

Saprophyte – an organism that takes nourishment from dead or decaying organic matter.

Scabers – tufted hairs or short projecting scales on stalk.

Shelf-like – without a stalk, generally growing from woody surfaces.

Species – a particular kind of organism; the fundamental unit of taxonomy.

Spines – pendant spore-bearing 'teeth' in the teeth fungi.

Spore – the reproductive unit of a fungus.

Stipe – the stem or stalk of a mushroom.

Substrate – the material to which a fruiting body is attached.

Symbiont – an organism that lives in a mutually beneficial relationship, or symbiosis, with another organism.

Terrestrial – growing from the ground.

Tube – a hollow cylinder in which spores are produced in boletes and polypores.

Universal veil – a tissue that encloses the entire immature stage of some mushrooms.

Veil – a tissue that covers and protects the immature stage of some mushrooms. Referred to as a universal veil when it encloses the entire immature mushroom; a partial veil when it covers only the gills or tubes.

Volva – a sac-like cup of tissue surrounding the stalk base, left after the universal veil has ruptured.

Mushroom Nomenclature[22]

"SPRING SURPRISES"

black morel: *Morchella elata*[23]
blonde (yellow) morel: *Morchella esculenta*
oyster musroom: *Pleurotus ostreatus*
green oyster: *Panellus serotinus*
flat crep: *Crepidotus applanatus*
angel wings: *Pleurocybella porrigens*
chicken mushroom: *Laetiporous sulphureus*
wine-cap: *Stropharia rugosoannulata*
garland stropharia: *Stropharia coronilla*

"SUMPTUOUS SUMMER FINDS"

the sickener: *Russula emetica*
variable Russula: *Russula variata*
green-quilt Russula: *Russula costosa*
corrugated cap milky: *Lactarius corrugis*
hygrophorous milky: *Lactarius hygrophoroides*
voluminous latex milky: *Lactarius volemus*
chanterelle: *Chantharellus cibarius*
smooth chanterelle: *Chantharellus lateritius*
red chanterelle: *Chantharellus cinnabarinus*
black trumpet: *Craterellus fallax*
horn of plenty: *Craterellus cornucopioides*
King bolete (porcini): *Boletus edulis*
two-colored bolete: *Boletus bicolor*
brick-cap bolete: *Boletus sensibilis*
common scaber stalk: *Leccinum scabrum*
black staining polypore: *Meripilus giganteus*
jack-o-lantern: *Omphalotus illudens*

---

22 All Latin names from the 2006 printing of the National Audubon Society field guide to mushrooms
23 Note that the genus is always capitalized and the species is not. Although I have not done this, where the genus is repeated it is common to use only the first letter of the genus, e.g., M. esculenta

"AUTUMN ADVENTURES"

big laughing gym: *Gymnopilus spectabilis*
honey mushroom: *Armillaria mellea*
golden Pholiota: *Pholiota aurivella*
deadly Galerina: *Galerina autumnalis*
hen of the woods: *Grifola frondosa*
brick tops: *Nematoloma sublateritium*
sulfur tuft: *Nematoloma fasciculare*

"OTHER DELECTABLE GOODIES"

sweet tooth (hedgehog): *Dentinum repandum*
bear's head tooth: *Hericium coralloides*
fried chicken mushroom: *Lyophyllum decastes*
beefsteak mushroom: *Fistulina hepatica*
red-capped scaber stalk: *Leccinum aurantiacum*

"ABOUT POISONOUS MUSHROOMS"

destroying angel: *Amanita virosa*
death-cap: *Amanita phalloides*
deadly Cort: *Cortinarius gentilis*
fly agaric: *Amanita muscaria*

Bibliography

Mushrooms Demystified; David Arora

National Audubon Society Field Guide to Mushrooms; Gary Lincoff, President NAMA

Edible Wild Mushrooms of North America; Fischer and Bessette

North American Boletes; Bessette, Roody and Bessette

Peterson Field Guide: Mushrooms; McKnight and McKnight

Mushrooms of the World; Giuseppe Pace

The Ultimate Mushroom Book; Jordan and Wheeler

A Cook's Book of Mushrooms; Czarnecki